Energy Tax Incentives: Measuring Value Across Different Types of Energy Resources

Molly F. Sherlock
Specialist in Public Finance

September 18, 2012

Congressional Research Service
7-5700
www.crs.gov
R41953

CRS Report for Congress
Prepared for Members and Committees of Congress

Summary

The majority of energy produced in the United States is derived from fossil fuels. In recent years, however, revenue losses associated with tax incentives that benefit renewables have exceeded revenue losses associated with tax incentives benefitting fossil fuels. As Congress evaluates the tax code and various energy tax incentives, there has been interest in understanding how energy tax benefits under the current tax system are distributed across different domestic energy resources.

In 2010, fossil fuels accounted for 78.0% of U.S. primary energy production. The remaining primary energy production is attributable to nuclear electric and renewable energy resources, with shares of 11.2% and 10.7%, respectively. Primary energy production using renewable energy resources includes both electricity generated using renewable resources, including hydropower, as well as renewable fuels (e.g., biofuels).

The value of federal tax support for the energy sector was estimated to be $19.1 billion in 2010. Of this, roughly one-third ($6.3 billion) was for tax incentives that support renewable fuels. Another $6.7 billion can be attributed to tax-related incentives supporting various renewable energy technologies (e.g., wind and solar). Targeted tax incentives supporting fossil energy resources totaled $2.4 billion.

This report provides an analysis of the value of energy tax incentives relative to primary energy production levels. Relative to their share in overall energy production, renewables receive more federal financial support through the tax code than energy produced using fossil energy resources. Within the renewable energy sector, relative to the level of energy produced, biofuels receive the most tax-related financial support.

The report also summarizes the results of recently published studies by the Energy Information Administration (EIA) evaluating energy subsidies across various technologies. According to data presented in the EIA reports, the share of direct federal financial support for electricity produced using coal, natural gas and petroleum, and nuclear energy resources was similar in 2007 and 2010. Between 2007 and 2010, however, the share of federal financial support for electricity produced by renewables increased substantially, and federal financial support for refined coal disappeared.

Projections of the annual cost of energy-related tax provisions through 2015 show that, under current law, tax-related support for renewable fuels will effectively disappear after 2012. The amount of tax-related support for renewable electricity is also scheduled to decline over time given the recent expiration of the Section 1603 grants in lieu of tax credits program and the scheduled expiration of other tax incentives for renewable electricity, such as the production tax credit (PTC). The value of energy-related tax provisions that benefit fossil fuels is projected to remain relatively constant over time, under current law, as most provisions that benefit fossil fuels are permanent Internal Revenue Code (IRC) provisions.

Contents

Tax Incentives Relative to Energy Production 2
    Limitations of the Analysis 2
    Energy Production 3
    Energy Tax Incentives 5
    Fossil Fuels Versus Renewables: Relative Production and Tax Incentive Levels 8
    Projected Changes in Energy Tax Incentive Trends 10
Subsidies Relative to Production: The Energy Information Administration (EIA) Studies 13
Concluding Remarks 19
        What Is an "Effective" Tax Rate 21
        Effective Tax Rates for Energy-Related Capital Investments 21

Figures

Figure 1. Primary Energy Production by Source 5
Figure 2. Projected Annual Cost of Energy-Related Tax Incentives 11
Figure 3. Projected Cost of Energy Tax Provisions: FY2011 and FY2015 13

Tables

Table 1. Primary Energy Production by Source 4
Table 2. Estimated Revenue Cost of Energy Tax Provisions: Fiscal Years 2010 through
    2012 6
Table 3. Comparing Energy Production and Energy Tax Incentives: Fossil Fuels and
    Renewables 8
Table 4. Subsidies to Electricity Production by Fuel Type, 2010 15
Table 5. Subsidies to Electricity Production by Fuel Type, 2007 16
Table 6. Energy Subsidies Not Related to Electricity Production, 2010 17
Table 7. Energy Subsidies Not Related to Electricity Production, 2007 18
Table A-1. Comparing Energy Production and Energy Tax Incentives: Fossil Fuels and
    Renewables 20
Table B-1. Effective Tax Rates for Energy-Related Capital Investments 22

Appendixes

Appendix A. Comparing Energy Production to Energy Tax Incentives: 2009 20
Appendix B. An Alternative Method for Evaluating the Value of Energy Tax Incentives
    Across Technologies: The Effective Tax Rate Approach 21

Contacts

Author Contact Information..23

Since the 1970s, policymakers have increasingly used the tax code to promote energy policy goals. Historically, the majority of revenue losses associated with energy tax incentives have resulted from provisions benefitting fossil fuels. At present, the balance has shifted, such that the bulk of federal revenue losses associated with energy tax provisions are from incentives for renewable energy.[1]

While costs associated with energy tax policy have shifted towards incentives that promote renewable energy, the majority of domestic energy produced continues to be from fossil energy resources. This has raised questions regarding the value of energy tax incentives relative to production, and the relative subsidization of various energy resources.

The 112th Congress has considered legislation that would change the energy tax landscape. Specifically, the Close Big Oil Tax Loopholes Act (S. 940) proposes to eliminate various oil and gas tax incentives for major integrated oil companies.[2] Whether to extend certain expired and expiring energy tax provisions—e.g., the Section 1603 grants in lieu of tax credits and the production tax credit (PTC) for wind—has also been an issue considered by the 112th Congress (see the Family and Business Tax Cut Certainty Act of 2012).[3] As Congress continues to evaluate tax reform in the context of deficit reduction, they may consider whether various energy-related tax incentives should be extended, scaled back, or otherwise modified.

This report provides background information that might be useful as Congress continues to evaluate current energy tax policy. Specifically, the report presents a comparison of the cost of tax incentives associated with fossil and renewable energy resources, relative to amount of energy produced using each type of resource. The report also reviews other analyses that compare the cost of energy tax incentives relative to production, across different types of energy technologies.

Although the numbers in this report may be useful for policymakers evaluating the current status of energy tax policy, it is important to understand the limitations of this analysis. This report evaluates energy production relative to the value of current energy tax expenditures. It does not, however, seek to analyze whether the current system of energy tax incentives is economically efficient, effective, or otherwise consistent with broader energy policy objectives.[4] Further, analysis in this report does not include information on federal spending on energy that is not linked to the tax code.[5]

---

[1] For historical revenue losses associated with energy tax incentives, see CRS Report R41227, *Energy Tax Policy: Historical Perspectives on and Current Status of Energy Tax Expenditures*, by Molly F. Sherlock.

[2] S. 940 failed to advance in a May 16, 2011, vote in the Senate.

[3] Background materials related to consideration of the Family Business and Tax Cut Certainty Act of 2012 are available through the Senate Finance Committee website: http://www.finance.senate.gov/legislation/details/?id=1cb48bce-5056-a032-5255-272274d52b64. The Repeal Big Oil Tax Subsidies Act (S. 2204) also proposed extending certain temporary energy-related tax incentives, limiting a number of other tax provisions for major integrated oil companies.

[4] For a discussion of an economic framework for evaluating energy tax incentives, see CRS Report R41769, *Energy Tax Policy: Issues in the 112th Congress*, by Molly F. Sherlock and Margot L. Crandall-Hollick and U.S. Congress, Joint Committee on Taxation, Tax Expenditures for Energy Production and Conservation, committee print, 111th Cong., April 21, 2009, JCX-25-09R.

[5] This report does present data from the Energy Information Administration on total targeted federal financial support for energy. For a comprehensive review of federal financial support for energy, see U.S. Energy Information Administration, *Direct Federal Financial Interventions and Subsidies in Energy in Fiscal Year 2010*, Washington, DC, July 2011, http://www.eia.gov.

Tax Incentives Relative to Energy Production

The following sections estimate the value of tax incentives relative to the level of energy produced using fossil and renewable energy resources. Before proceeding with the analysis, some limitations are outlined. The analysis itself requires quantification of energy production and energy tax incentives. Once data on energy production and energy tax incentives have been presented, the value of energy tax incentives can be evaluated relative to current levels of energy production.

Limitations of the Analysis

The analysis below provides a broad comparison of the relative tax support for fossil fuels as compared to the relative support for renewables. Various data limitations prevent a precise analysis of the amount of subsidy per unit of production across different energy resources. Limitations associated with this type of analysis include the following:

- **Current-year tax incentives may not directly support current-year production**

    Many of the tax incentives available for energy resources are designed to encourage investment, rather than production. For example, the expensing of intangible drilling costs (IDCs) for oil and gas provides an incentive to invest in capital equipment and exploration. Although the ability to expense IDCs does not directly support current production of crude oil and natural gas, such subsidies are expected to increase long-run supply.

- **Differing levels of federal financial support may or may not reflect policy rationale**

    Various policy rationales may exist for federal interventions in energy markets. Interventions may be designed to achieve various economic, social, or other policy objectives. Although analysis of federal financial support per unit of energy production may help inform the policy debate, it does not directly consider why various energy sources may receive different levels of federal financial support.

- **Tax expenditures are estimates**

    The tax expenditure data provided by the Joint Committee on Taxation (JCT) are estimates of federal revenue loss associated with a specific provision.[6] These estimates do not provide information on actual federal revenue losses, nor do these estimates reflect the amount of revenue that would be raised should the provision be eliminated.[7]

- **Tax expenditure data are not specific to energy source**

    Many tax incentives are available to a variety of energy resources. For example, the tax expenditure associated with the expensing of IDCs does not distinguish

---

[6] These caveats also apply to the annual tax expenditure estimates provided by the Treasury Department.

[7] Data on the actual revenue losses associated with various provisions are generally not publicly available.

between revenue losses associated with natural gas versus those associated with oil. The tax expenditure for five-year accelerated depreciation also does not specify how much of the benefit accrues to various eligible technologies, such as wind and solar.

- **A number of tax provisions that support energy are not energy specific**

    The U.S. energy sector benefits from a number of tax provisions that are not targeted at energy. For example, the production activities deduction (§ 199) benefits all domestic manufacturers. For the purposes of the § 199 deduction, oil and gas extraction is considered a domestic manufacturing activity.[8] Certain energy-related activities may also benefit from other tax incentives that are available to non-energy industries, such as the ability to issue tax-exempt debt,[9] the ability to structure as a master limited partnership,[10] or tax incentives designed to promote other activities, such as research and development.

Energy Production

The Energy Information Administration (EIA) provides annual data on U.S. primary energy production. EIA defines primary energy as energy that exists in a naturally occurring form, before being converted into an end-use product. For example, coal is considered primary energy, which can be converted to synthetic gas and later electricity.[11]

This report relies on 2010 data on U.S. primary energy production (see **Table 1** and **Figure 1**).[12] Coal and natural gas are the two largest primary energy production sources, each representing 29.4% of primary energy production in 2010. Crude oil constituted 15.6% of primary energy production.[13] Taken together, fossil energy sources were used for 78.0% of 2010 primary energy production.

The remaining U.S. primary energy production is attributable to nuclear electric and renewable energy resources. Overall, 11.2% of 2010 U.S. primary energy was produced as nuclear electric energy. Renewables (including hydro-electric power) constituted 10.7% of 2010 U.S. primary energy production. Excluding hydro-electric power, renewable energy resources constituted approximately 7.4% of primary energy production in 2010.

---

[8] The Emergency Economic Stabilization Act of 2008 (EESA; P.L. 110-343) permanently limited oil and gas extraction to a 6% deduction. Other qualified activities may claim a 9% deduction.

[9] For more information on subsidized debt financing for energy, see CRS Report R41573, *Tax-Favored Financing for Renewable Energy Resources and Energy Efficiency*, by Molly F. Sherlock and Steven Maguire.

[10] For additional background, see CRS Report R41893, *Master Limited Partnerships: A Policy Option for the Renewable Energy Industry*, by Molly F. Sherlock and Mark P. Keightley.

[11] Definitions and data can be found in Energy Information Administration, *Annual Energy Review, 2010*, Washington, DC, October 19, 2011, http://www.eia.gov/totalenergy/data/annual/index.cfm.

[12] 2010 is the most recent year available. These figures are preliminary and may be subject to revision.

[13] The figures for primary energy consumption differ from those for primary energy production. For example, while crude oil was the source for 15.6% of primary energy production in 2010, 36.7% of primary energy consumed was attributed to petroleum. Much of this difference reflects U.S. reliance on imported petroleum.

Table 1. Primary Energy Production by Source
2010

Source	Quadrillion Btu[a]	Percent of Total
Fossil Fuels		
Coal	22.1	29.4%
Natural Gas	22.1	29.4%
Crude Oil	11.7	15.6%
Natural Gas Plant Liquids	2.7	3.6%
Nuclear		
Nuclear Electric	8.4	11.2%
Renewable Energy		
Hydro-Electric Power	2.5	3.3%
Geothermal	0.2	0.3%
Solar/PV	0.1	0.1%
Wind	0.9	1.2%
Biomass[b]	4.3	5.7%
Total	**75.0**	**100%**

Source: CRS analysis of data from Energy Information Administration, *Annual Energy Review, 2010*. Data are presented graphically in **Figure 1**.

Notes: Columns may not sum due to rounding.

a. A British thermal unit (Btu) is the amount of heat required to raise the temperature of one pound of water 1 degree Fahrenheit.

b. Within the biomass category, 1.9 quadrillion Btu attributed to biofuels. Biofuels constituted 2.5% of total primary energy production in 2010.

Biomass was the largest source of production amongst the renewables in 2010, accounting for 5.7% of overall primary energy production or more than half of renewable energy production. This was followed by hydro-electric power at 3.3% of primary energy production. The remaining three resources, wind, geothermal, and solar were responsible for 1.2%, 0.3%, and 0.1% of 2009 primary energy production, respectively (see **Table 1** and **Figure 1**).

Primary energy produced using biomass can be further categorized as biomass being used to produce biofuels (e.g., ethanol) and biomass being used to generate biopower.[14] Of the 4.3 quadrillion Btu of energy produced using biomass, nearly 1.9 quadrillion Btu, or 43.4%, was used in the production of biofuels.[15,16]

---

[14] It is unclear whether biopower is carbon neutral. For background on this debate, see CRS Report R41603, *Is Biopower Carbon Neutral?* by Kelsi Bracmort. For more information on biofuels, see CRS Report R41282, *Agriculture-Based Biofuels: Overview and Emerging Issues*, by Randy Schnepf and CRS Report R40110, *Biofuels Incentives: A Summary of Federal Programs*, by Brent D. Yacobucci. For more information on biopower, see CRS Report R41440, *Biomass Feedstocks for Biopower: Background and Selected Issues*, by Kelsi Bracmort.

[15] Biofuels includes wood and wood-derived fuels, biomass waste, and total biomass inputs to the production of fuel ethanol and biodiesel.

[16] A British thermal unit is the amount of heat required to raise the temperature of one pound of water one degree (continued...)

Figure 1. Primary Energy Production by Source
2010

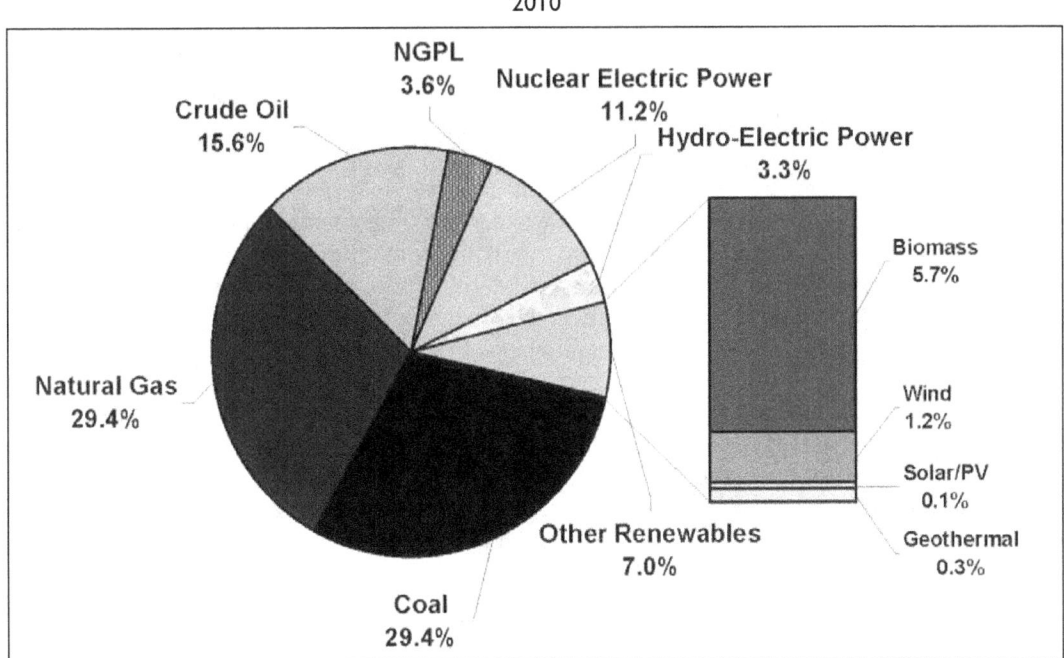

Source: CRS graphic using data from the Energy Information Administration, *Annual Energy Review, 2010*.

Notes: NGPL are Natural Gas Plant Liquids. Percentages may not sum to 100% due to rounding.

Energy Tax Incentives

The tax code supports the energy sector by providing a number of targeted tax incentives, or tax incentives only available for the energy industry. In addition to targeted tax incentives, the energy sector may also benefit from a number of broader tax provisions that are available for energy and non-energy-related taxpayers.[17] These broader tax incentives are not included in the analysis, since tax expenditure estimates do not indicate how much of the revenue loss associated with these generally available provisions is associated with energy-related activities.

Joint Committee on Taxation (JCT) tax expenditure estimates are used to tabulate federal revenue losses associated with energy tax provisions.[18] The tax expenditure estimates provided by the JCT are forecasted revenue losses. These revenue losses are not re-estimated on the basis of actual

---

(...continued)
Fahrenheit.

[17] For example, oil and gas producers currently benefit from the Section 199 domestic production deduction. This incentive is available to all domestic manufacturers, and is not specifically targeted towards the oil and gas sector.

[18] The Congressional Budget and Impoundment Act of 1974 (the Budget Act; P.L. 93-344) defines tax expenditures as "revenue losses attributable to provisions of the federal tax laws which allow a special exclusion, exemption, or deduction from gross income or which provide a special credit, a preferential rate of tax, or a deferral of tax liability." JCT is the official scorekeeper for congressional budget purposes. The Treasury also provides a list of tax expenditures annually.

economic conditions. Thus, revenue losses presented below are projected, as opposed to actual revenue losses.

The JCT advises that individual tax expenditures cannot be simply summed to estimate the aggregate revenue loss from multiple tax provisions. This is because of interaction effects. When the revenue loss associated with a specific tax provision is estimated, the estimate is made assuming that there are no changes in other provisions or in taxpayer behavior. When individual tax expenditures are summed, the interaction effects may lead to different revenue loss estimates. Consequently, aggregate tax expenditure estimates, derived from summing the estimated revenue effects of individual tax expenditure provisions, are unlikely to reflect the actual change in federal receipts associated with removing various tax provisions.[19] Thus, total tax expenditure figures presented below are an estimate of federal revenue losses associated with energy tax provisions, and should not be interpreted as actual federal revenue losses.

Table 2 provides information on revenue losses and outlays associated with energy-related tax provisions during 2010, 2011, and 2012.[20] In 2010, the tax code provided an estimated $19.1 billion in support for the energy sector. In 2011, the estimated amount of support was $21.8 billion. For 2012, the estimated cost of tax-related support for energy is $16.6 billion. Much of the decline between 2011 and 2012 can be explained by the expiration of tax incentives for alcohol fuels which primarily supported ethanol.[21]

Table 2. Estimated Revenue Cost of Energy Tax Provisions: Fiscal Years 2010 through 2012

$ billions

Provision	2010	2011	2012
Fossil Fuels			
Expensing of Exploration and Development Costs for Oil and Gas	0.7	0.8	0.8
Percentage Depletion for Oil and Gas	0.5	0.9	0.9
Amortization of Geological and Geophysical Costs for Oil and Gas Exploration	0.1	0.1	0.1
15-year Depreciation for Natural Gas Distribution Lines	0.1	0.1	0.1
Election to Expense 50% of Qualified Refinery Costs	0.7	0.8	0.7
Amortization of Air Pollution Control Facilities	0.1	0.2	0.2
Credits for Investments in Clean Coal Facilities	0.2	0.2	0.2

---

[19] See CRS Report RL33641, *Tax Expenditures: Trends and Critiques*, by Thomas L. Hungerford and U.S. Congress, Senate Committee on the Budget, *Tax Expenditures: Compendium of Background Material on Individual Provisions*, committee print, prepared by Congressional Research Service, 111th Cong., 2nd sess., December 2010, [henceforth referenced as the "2010 Tax Expenditure Compendium"].

[20] Energy-related tax provisions are those listed under the "Energy" heading in the Joint Committee on Taxation's annual tax expenditure list. Although technically not tax expenditures, the cost associated with excise tax credits and outlays under the Section 1603 grants in lieu of tax credits program are also included in **Table 2**.

[21] Tax incentives for alcohol fuels, including the volumetric ethanol excise tax credit (VEETC), were allowed to expire at the end of calendar year 2011. As reported in **Table 2**, excise tax incentives for alcohol fuels in FY2012 have an estimated cost of $3.6 billion. Part of this cost is for claims made in the last quarter of calendar year 2011, thus showing up in FY2012. Part of this cost in FY2012 is also explained by claims made related to calendar year 2011 that were not processed until FY2012.

Provision	2010	2011	2012
Excise Tax Credits for Alternative Fuel Mixtures	n.a.	0.2	0.2
Subtotal, Fossil Fuels	*2.4*	*3.3*	*3.2*
Renewables			
Production Tax Credit (PTC)	1.4	1.4	1.6
Investment Tax Credit (ITC)	(i)	0.5	0.5
Accelerated Depreciation for Renewable Energy Property	0.3	0.3	0.3
Section 1603 Grants in Lieu of Tax Credits[a]	4.2	3.5	4.1
Credit for Clean Renewable Energy Bonds (CREBs)	0.1	(i)	(i)
Residential Energy Efficient Property Credit	0.2	0.2	0.2
Credit for Investment in Advanced Energy Property	0.5	0.7	0.4
Subtotal, Renewables	*6.7*	*6.6*	*7.1*
Renewable Fuels			
Credits for Alcohol Fuels	0.1	0.2	0.1
Excise Tax Credits for Alcohol Fuels[a]	5.7	6.5	3.6
Excise Tax Credits for Biodiesel[a]	0.5	0.8	0.2
Subtotal, Renewable Fuels	*6.3*	*7.5*	*3.9*
Efficiency & Conservation			
Energy Efficiency Improvements to Existing Homes	1.7	1.5	1.3
Credit for Production of Energy Efficient Appliances	0.2	0.2	0.1
Energy Efficient Commercial Building Deduction	0.2	0.2	0.2
10-year Depreciation for Smart Electric Distribution Property	(i)	0.1	0.1
Subtotal, Efficiency & Conservation	*2.1*	*2.0*	*1.7*
Alternative Technology Vehicles			
Credits for Alternative Technology Vehicles	0.8	(i)	(i)
Credit for Plug-In Electric Vehicles	n.a.	0.1	0.3
Subtotal, Alternative Technology Vehicles	*0.8*	*0.1*	*0.3*
Other			
Percentage Depletion for Other Fuels	0.2	0.2	0.2
15-year Depreciation for Electric Transmission Property	0.1	0.1	0.2
Exceptions for Publicly Traded Partnerships with Qualified Income from Energy-Related Activities	0.5	0.2	0.2
Special Rule to Implement Electric Transmission Restructuring	(i)	1.8	-0.2
Subtotal, Other	*0.8*	*2.3*	*0.4*
Total	**19.1**	**21.8**	**16.6**

Source: Joint Committee on Taxation and the Department of the Treasury.

Notes: (i) indicates a positive estimated revenue loss of less than $50 million. An n.a. indicates that the provision was not listed in the 2010 tax expenditure tables. Provisions with a revenue score of less than $50 million during 2010 and 2011 are omitted from the table.

a. The figures reported for the Section 1603 grants in lieu of tax credits and the excise tax credits for alcohol fuels and biodiesel are outlays as reported in the President's budget.

The largest energy-related provisions, in terms of federal revenue loss, over the 2010 through 2012 period, have both been allowed to expire. Between 2010 and 2012, the Section 1603 grants in lieu of tax credits program cost $11.8 billion. Over the same time period, excise tax credits for alcohol fuels cost $15.8 billion.[22] Both of these provisions expired at the end of 2011.[23] The expiration of a number of energy-related tax incentives means that, under current law, a substantial shift in balance of energy tax incentives across different types of energy resources is projected to occur (see the section "Projected Changes in Energy Tax Incentive Trends" below).

In 2010, tax incentives for renewables (including renewable electricity and renewable fuels) constituted an estimated 68.1% of the estimated total revenue loss associated with energy tax provisions.[24] Revenue losses associated with fossil-fuels-related tax incentives were an estimated $2.4 billion, or 12.6% of the estimated cost of energy tax incentives.

Fossil Fuels Versus Renewables: Relative Production and Tax Incentive Levels

Table 3 provides a side-by-side comparison of fossil fuel and renewable production, along with the cost of tax incentives supporting the two types of energy resources. During 2010, 78.0% of U.S. primary energy production could be attributed to fossil fuel sources. Of the federal tax support targeted to energy in 2010, an estimated 12.6% of the value of tax incentives went towards supporting fossil fuels. During 2010, an estimated 10.7% of U.S. primary source energy was produced using renewable resources. Of the federal tax support targeted to energy in 2010, an estimated 68.1% went towards supporting renewables.

Table 3. Comparing Energy Production and Energy Tax Incentives: Fossil Fuels and Renewables

2010

	Production		Tax Incentives	
	Quadrillion Btu	% of Total	Billions of Dollars	% of Total
Fossil Fuels	58.5	78.0%	$2.4	12.6%
Renewables[a]	8.1	10.7%	$13.0	68.1%

---

[22] Most of the revenue loss here can be attributed to the Volumetric Ethanol Excise Tax Credit (VEETC).

[23] The Section 1603 grants in lieu of tax credits program is only available for projects that were under construction prior to the end of 2011. Since grants are paid out when eligible property is placed in service, outlays under this program will continue for a number of years.

[24] The remainder of the analysis uses data from 2010, as this is the most recent year for which primary source energy production data are available.

	Production		Tax Incentives	
	Quadrillion Btu	% of Total	Billions of Dollars	% of Total
Renewables (excluding hydro-electric)	5.6	7.4%	$13.0[b]	68.1%[b]
Renewables (excluding biofuels and related tax incentives)	6.2	8.3%	$6.7	35.1%
Renewables (excluding hydro-electric and biofuels and related tax incentives)	3.7	4.9%	$6.7[b]	35.1%[b]

Source: Calculated using data presented in **Table 1** and **Table 2** above.

a. Renewables tax incentives include targeted tax incentives designed to support renewable electricity and renewable fuels.

b. The value of total tax incentives for renewables excluding hydro-electric power is less than the total value of tax incentives when those available for hydro-power are included. However, the difference is small. JCT estimates that in 2010, the tax expenditures for qualified hydropower under the PTC are less than $50 million. During 2010, two awards totaling $88,000 were paid to hydropower facilities under the Section 1603 grant program. Hydropower has also received less in CREB financing than was awarded to solar and wind technologies. During 2010, the tax expenditure for CREBs was an estimated $0.1 billion across all technologies.

One could argue that energy generated using hydro-electric power technologies should be excluded from the analysis, since most of today's hydro-generating capacity was established in the past (84% of today's hydro-electric generating capacity was installed before 1980; 99% was installed before 1996).[25] Thus, there is no clear federal tax benefit for most electricity currently generated using hydropower. Further, with most of the best hydro sites already developed, there is limited potential for growth in conventional hydropower capacity.[26] Nonetheless, there is potential for development of additional electricity-generating capacity through smaller hydro projects that could substantially increase U.S. hydro-electric generation capacity.[27] Excluding hydro from the renewables category, non-hydro renewables accounted for 7.4% of 2010 primary energy production.

During 2010, certain tax expenditures for renewable energy did, however, benefit taxpayers developing and operating hydro-electric power facilities. Specifically, development of hydro-electric facilities has been supported with clean renewable energy bonds (CREBs) and Section 1603 grants in lieu of tax credits.[28] Additionally, certain hydro-electric installations may be eligible for the renewable energy production tax credit (PTC) or the Section 1603 grants in lieu of

---

[25] Energy Information Administration, *Hydropower has a Long History in the United States,* July 8, 2011, available at http://www.eia.gov/todayinenergy/detail.cfm?id=2130.

[26] See CRS Report R41493, *Options for a Federal Renewable Electricity Standard*, by Richard J. Campbell.

[27] See CRS Report R41089, *Small Hydro and Low-Head Hydro Power Technologies and Prospects*, by Richard J. Campbell.

[28] For additional information on which technologies have benefitted from CREBs, see CRS Report R41573, *Tax-Favored Financing for Renewable Energy Resources and Energy Efficiency*, by Molly F. Sherlock and Steven Maguire. For additional information on which technologies have benefitted from the Section 1603 grants in lieu of tax credits program, see CRS Report R41635, *ARRA Section 1603 Grants in Lieu of Tax Credits for Renewable Energy: Overview, Analysis, and Policy Options*, by Phillip Brown and Molly F. Sherlock.

tax credits program.[29] Given that hydro is supported by 2010 tax expenditures, one could also argue that hydro should not be excluded from the renewables category. Rather, it could be said that hydro is demonstrative of the timing problem in trying to calculate the value of tax incentives per unit of energy production, as current hydro-related energy tax expenditures are not directly related to current hydro-electric production.

In 2010, nearly half of the tax incentives for renewables benefitted biofuels. Of the estimated $19.1 billion in energy tax provisions in 2010, an estimated $6.3 billion, or 33.0%, went toward supporting biofuels. Excluding tax incentives for biofuels, 35.1% of energy-related tax incentives in 2010 were attributable to renewables. In other words, excluding biofuels from the analysis reduces the share of tax incentives attributable to renewables from 68.1% to 35.1%. Excluding biofuels from the analysis has a smaller impact on renewables' share of primary energy production. When biofuels are excluded, the share of primary energy produced in 2010 attributable to renewables falls by 2.4 percentage points, from 10.7% to 8.3%.[30]

Projected Changes in Energy Tax Incentive Trends

Over time, there have been substantial shifts in the proportion of energy-related tax expenditures benefitting different types of energy resources (see **Figure 2**). Beginning in the mid-2000s, the cost of energy tax incentives for renewables began to increase. From 2009 onwards, the increased costs associated with incentives for renewable electricity are largely attributable to the Section 1603 grants in lieu of tax credit program.[31] The Section 1603 grant option is not available for projects that began construction after December 31, 2011. However, since grants are paid out when construction is completed and eligible property is placed in service, outlays under the Section 1603 program are expected to continue through 2017.[32]

From the 1980s through 2010, most of the tax-related federal financial support for renewable energy was for renewable fuels, mainly alcohol fuels (i.e., ethanol).[33] Starting in 2008, the federal

---

[29] In 2010, two Section 1603 grants totaling $88,000 were awarded to hydropower projects. As of July 2012, a total of $33 million in Section 1603 grants has been paid out to qualifying hydropower facilities. A complete list of Section 1603 grant recipients is available from the Department of Treasury, at http://www.treasury.gov/initiatives/recovery/Pages/1603.aspx.

[30] The data in **Table 3** can be used to provide an estimate of federal tax support per million Btu produced using fossil fuel and renewable energy resources. Such analysis, however, does not directly link the amount of federal financial support given directly to energy produced, as many federal tax incentives for energy reward investments rather than production. In other words, current federal financial incentives do not directly support current energy production. From this perspective, evaluating the current value of federal financial support per Btu of energy production is methodologically flawed. Nonetheless, this type of analysis has been used in the past. For example, see the 2007 EIA study discussed in greater detail below.

[31] For additional background, see CRS Report R41635, *ARRA Section 1603 Grants in Lieu of Tax Credits for Renewable Energy: Overview, Analysis, and Policy Options*, by Phillip Brown and Molly F. Sherlock.

[32] Outlays under the Section 1603 grant program are projected to be $4.1 billion for FY2012. Under current law, wind property must be placed in service prior to the end of calendar year 2012 to qualify for the Section 1603 grant. To qualify for the grant, eligible biomass, geothermal energy, landfill gas, trash, hydropower, and marine and hydrokinetic property must be placed in service by the end of 2013. By FY2015, outlays under the Section 1603 grant program are projected to fall to $1.2 billion. The placed-in-service deadline for solar, geothermal heat pump, fuel cell, microturbine, and combined heat and power (CHP) property is the end of 2016. For FY2017, projected outlays are $0.1 billion.

[33] The dramatic increase in estimated revenue losses in 2009 for renewable fuels was due to "black liquor." For more information, see CRS Report R41769, *Energy Tax Policy: Issues in the 112th Congress*, by Molly F. Sherlock and Margot L. Crandall-Hollick.

government incurred outlays associated with excise tax credits for biodiesel and renewable diesel. The tax credits for alcohol fuels (including ethanol) as well as the tax credits for biodiesel and renewable diesel expired at the end of 2011. Thus, after 2012, under current law, there are no projected costs associated with tax incentives for renewable fuels.[34]

Revenue losses for tax incentives supporting energy efficiency are also projected to decline in 2013, relative to revenue losses for efficiency-related provisions from 2008 through 2012. Most of the increase in revenue losses for efficiency-related provisions was associated with tax incentives for homeowners investing in certain energy-efficient property.[35] The primary tax incentive for energy efficiency improvements to existing homes expired at the end of 2011.[36] Extension of expired tax incentives for energy efficiency would increase the cost of energy efficiency-related tax incentives.

Figure 2. Projected Annual Cost of Energy-Related Tax Incentives
FY1977 - FY2015

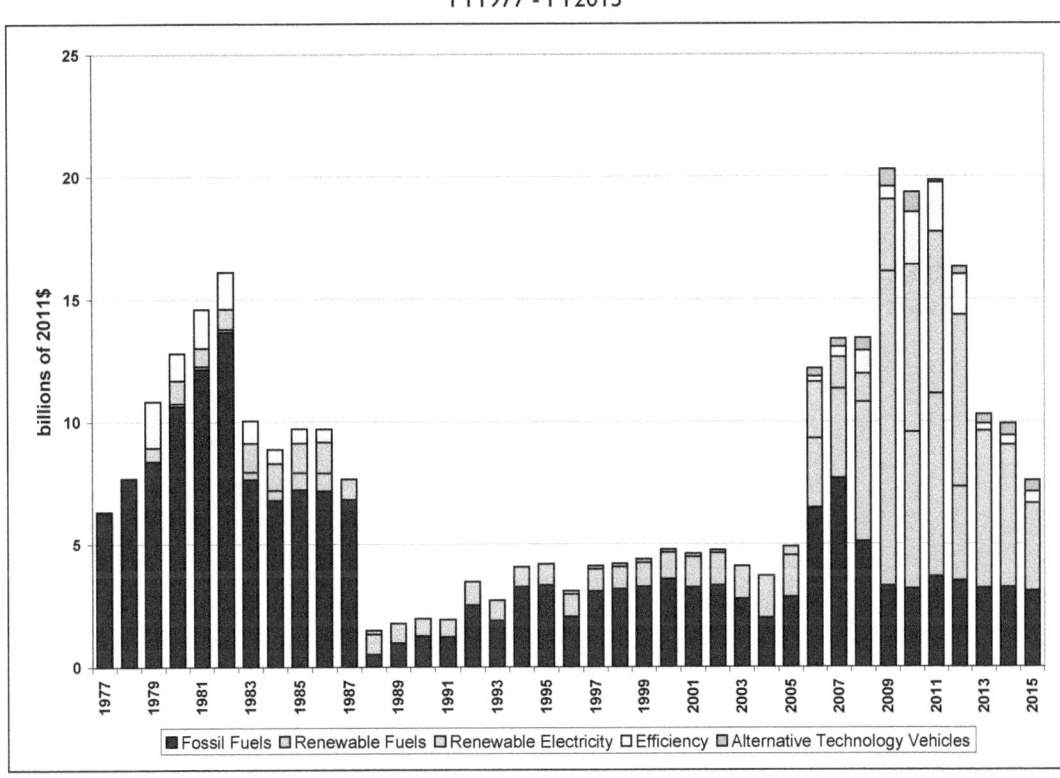

Source: CRS using data from the Joint Committee on Taxation and Office of Management and Budget.

Notes: Annual cost estimates are the sum of individual tax expenditure provisions and do not reflect possible interaction effects. The estimates also do not reflect the revenue that could be raised should specific provisions be eliminated. For all years, tax expenditure estimates are projections, not actual revenue losses. The figure does

---

[34] It is possible that there may continue to be revenue losses associated with tax incentives for renewable fuels beyond 2012 if taxpayers carry forward unused credits.

[35] For more information, see CRS Report R42089, *Residential Energy Tax Credits: Overview and Analysis*, by Margot L. Crandall-Hollick and Molly F. Sherlock.

[36] The nonbusiness energy property credit (Internal Revenue Code (IRC) § 25C) expired at the end of 2011.

not include energy-related tax expenditure provisions that cannot be attributed to a specific fuel or technology. The figure does include outlays associated with excise tax credits for alcohol fuels (e.g., ethanol), other biofuels and alternative fuels, and outlays for grants paid out under the Section 1603 program.

As was noted above, much of the projected cost of energy-related tax incentives in the out years is associated with expired or expiring provisions. Costs for certain provisions may extend beyond expiration for a number of reasons. In the case of the Section 1603 grant program, since outlays occur when property is placed in service, costs for this program will continue to be incurred long past its 2011 expiration date. Another example is the renewable energy production tax credit (PTC). The PTC is available for the first 10 years of production from a qualified facility. Thus, property placed in service in 2010 may claim production tax credits through 2020. Even with the PTC for wind scheduled to expire in 2012, wind energy facilities that were placed in service before December 31, 2012 may continue to receive tax credits through 2022. Revenue losses associated with tax provisions can also extend beyond a provision's expiration when taxpayers are allowed to carry forward unused tax credits, using credits to offset liability in future tax years.

Accounting for expired provisions has additional implications for trends in tax-related support for different types of energy resources. Between 2011 and 2015, the cost of tax-related provisions that support renewable energy is projected to decline from $6.6 billion to $3.6 billion (see **Figure 3**).[37] The majority of the $3.6 billion cost in 2015 is associated with the Section 1603 grant program, which expired in 2011, and the PTC for wind, which is scheduled to expire at the end of 2012. Thus, in 2015, these incentives will no longer be available for new investments in renewable electricity. Of the $3.6 billion projected cost for renewable electricity provisions in 2015, $2.8 billion is for expired incentives while $0.7 billion is for incentives available for new projects in 2015. Extension of certain tax incentives for renewable energy be extended, such as the production tax credit, would change this analysis.

---

[37] Projected costs for 2015 are inflation-adjusted to constant 2011 dollars.

Figure 3. Projected Cost of Energy Tax Provisions: FY2011 and FY2015
Changes Associated with Expiring Provisions

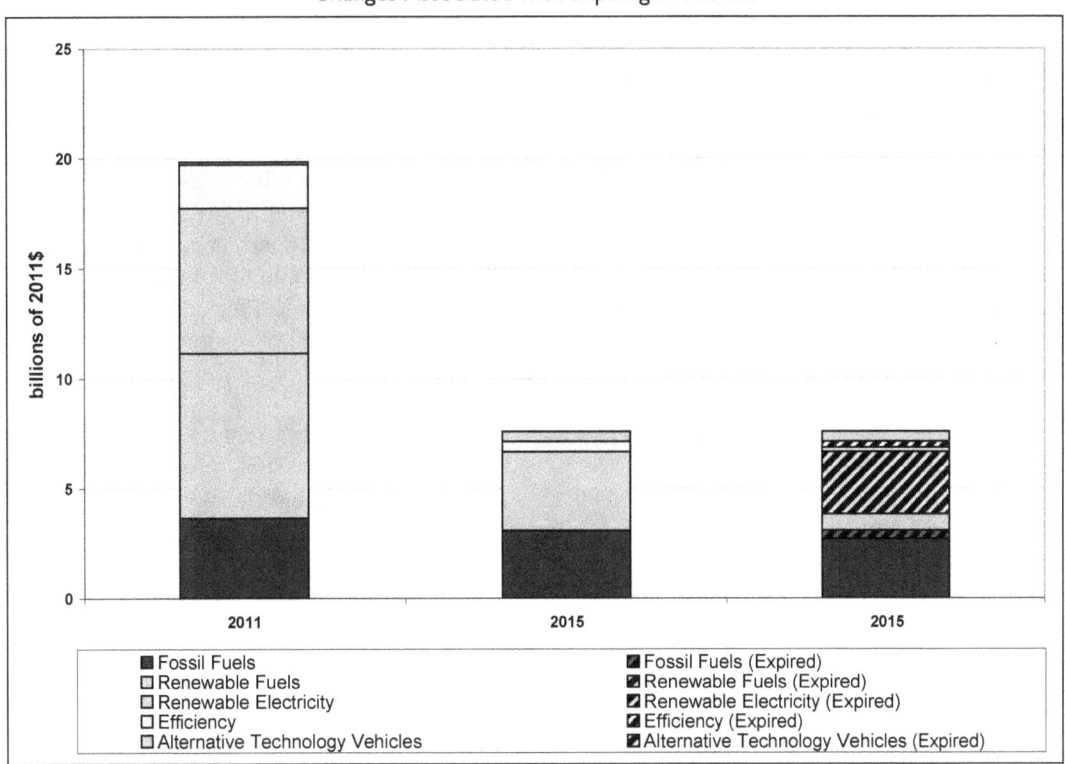

Source: CRS using data from the Joint Committee on Taxation and Office of Management and Budget.

Notes: Annual cost estimates are the sum of individual tax expenditure provisions and do not reflect possible interaction effects. The estimates also do not reflect the revenue that could be raised should specific provisions be eliminated. For all years, tax expenditure estimates are projections, not actual revenue losses. The figure does not include energy-related tax expenditure provisions that cannot be attributed to a specific fuel or technology. The figure does include outlays associated with excise tax credits for alcohol fuels (e.g., ethanol), other biofuels and alternative fuels, and outlays for grants paid out under the Section 1603 program.

For fossil fuels, the cost of energy-related tax provisions was roughly $3.7 billion in 2011 (see **Figure 3**). This cost is projected to be $3.1 billion in 2015. Most of the tax incentives that support fossil fuels are permanent features of the tax code, and thus are not scheduled to expire. This explains why the projected cost of tax provisions that support fossil fuels is expected to remain relatively steady over the next few years.

Subsidies Relative to Production: The Energy Information Administration (EIA) Studies

Other studies have examined federal financial support (e.g., "subsidies") across various energy resources. Some of this research is similar to what has been presented thus far, in that it examines federal financial support relative to energy produced across different energy sources. Using an alternative approach, other research has compared the subsidization of different energy resources using effective tax rates (see **Appendix B** for an overview of effective tax rate studies).[38]

In recent years, the Energy Information Administration (EIA) has released studies providing analysis of energy and electricity production subsidies.[39] In this work, the EIA defines subsidies to include spending and tax expenditure provisions. On the spending side, the EIA includes direct expenditures that result in payments to energy producers or consumers as well as energy-related federal research and development (R&D) funding. The EIA analysis also includes certain energy-related federal loan guarantees and federal electricity support programs in their tabulation of federal energy subsidies. On the tax side, the EIA study includes tax expenditures. The analysis presented above focuses exclusively on energy subsidies provided through the tax code, and does not examine spending-side energy subsidies. In contrast to the EIA studies, the analysis presented above includes Section 1603 grants in lieu of tax credits as a tax-related provision. EIA lists the Section 1603 grants in lieu of tax credits as a direct expenditure.

To estimate energy subsidies per unit of electricity production across different energy resources, the EIA employs the following methodology. First, the EIA defines electricity production that is supported by federal subsidies. Next, the analysis examines all energy subsidies, categorizing these subsidies into those that support electricity production and those that support other uses of energy. The analysis then allocates electricity-related energy subsidies by fuel type. Using this information on electricity production and federal subsidies, the EIA is able determine the share of electricity or energy attributable to a specific fuel, relative to the share of federal financial support received by that fuel. The results of EIA's analyses covering 2010 and 2007 are summarized in **Table 4** and **Table 5**, respectively.

For 2010 and 2007, coal was found to be the largest fuel source for electricity production, while receiving a relatively small share of federal financial support. Although 44.9% of 2010 generation can be attributed to coal, of total direct federal financial support for electricity production in 2010, coal received an estimated 10%. These figures are similar to EIA's findings for 2007, where 47.6% of generation was attributable to coal, while coal received 12.7% of the total federal financial support for electricity production.

---

[38] One drawback associated with the effective tax rate analysis presented in **Appendix B** is that it relies on tax parameters that were in place prior to the enactment of the American Recovery and Reinvestment Act of 2009 (ARRA; P.L. 111-5). ARRA contained a number of energy-related provisions, and substantially changed the nature of federal financial support for renewables. For additional information, see CRS Report R40412, *Energy Provisions in the American Recovery and Reinvestment Act of 2009 (P.L. 111-5)*, coordinated by Fred Sissine, CRS Report R41635, *ARRA Section 1603 Grants in Lieu of Tax Credits for Renewable Energy: Overview, Analysis, and Policy Options*, by Phillip Brown and Molly F. Sherlock, and CRS Report R40999, *Energy Tax Policy: Issues in the 111th Congress*, by Molly F. Sherlock and Donald J. Marples.

[39] The two EIA reports covered in this report are (1) Energy Information Administration, *Federal Financial Interventions and Subsidies in Energy Markets 2007*, Report #:SR/CNEAF/2008-01, Washington, DC, April 2008, http://www.eia.gov/oiaf/servicerpt/subsidy2/index.html, and (2) Energy Information Administration, *Direct Federal Financial Interventions and Subsidies in Energy in Fiscal Year 2010*, Washington, DC, July 2011, http://www.eia.gov/analysis/requests/subsidy/pdf/subsidy.pdf.

Table 4. Subsidies to Electricity Production by Fuel Type, 2010

dollar values in millions

Fuel Type	Production		Federal Financial Incentives		
	FY2010 Net Generation (billion kWh)	% of Total	Tax Subsidies	Other Subsidies[a]	% of Total
Coal	1,851	44.9%	486	703	10.0%
Natural Gas and Petroleum Liquids	1,030	25.0%	583	72	5.5%
Nuclear	807	19.6%	908	1,591	21.0%
Renewables	425	10.3%	1,347[b]	5,212[b]	55.3%
Biomass	57	1.4%	54	61	1.0%
Geothermal	16	0.4%	1	199	1.7%
Hydropower	257	6.2%	17	198	1.8%
Solar	1	0.0%	99	869	8.2%
Wind	95	2.3%	1,178	3,808	42.0%
Transmission and Distribution	-i-	-i-	58	924	8.2%
Total	**4,091**	**100%**	**3,382**	**8,502**	**100%**

Source: Energy Information Administration (EIA), Direct Federal Financial Interventions and Subsidies in Energy in Fiscal Year 2010.

Notes: An "-i-" indicates that the value was found as "not meaningful" by the EIA. Columns may not sum due to rounding.

a. Other subsidies include direct expenditures, research and development expenditures, federal electricity support, and loan guarantees.

b. The EIA includes the Section 1603 grants in lieu of tax credits in their direct expenditures category. The analysis above includes Section 1603 grants as tax-related federal financial support, since eligibility for Section 1603 grants is tied to the tax code. In 2010, $4.25 billion in Section 1603 grants in lieu of tax credits were awarded to renewable energy projects.

The shares of electricity produced using natural gas and petroleum as well as nuclear resources, and the share of federal financial support for electricity received by these resources, also remained similar between 2007 and 2010. In 2010 (2007), 25% (22.5%) of electricity production was attributable to natural gas and petroleum liquids. Of total direct federal financial support for electricity production in 2010, natural gas and petroleum liquids received an estimated 5.5% (3.4%). While the share of electricity produced using natural gas and petroleum is similar to the share of electricity produced using nuclear, relative to natural gas and petroleum it received a larger proportion of federal financial support for electricity in both 2007 and 2010. In 2010 (2007), the share of electricity produced using nuclear was 19.6% (19.4%), while the share of federal financial support was 21.0% (18.8%).

Table 5. Subsidies to Electricity Production by Fuel Type, 2007
dollar values in millions

Fuel Type	Production		Federal Financial Incentives		
	FY2007 Net Generation (billion kWh)	% of Total	Tax Subsidies	Other Subsidies[a]	% of Total
Coal	1,946	47.6%	264	590	12.7%
Refined Coal	72	1.8%	2,156		32.0%
Natural Gas and Petroleum Liquids	919	22.5%	203	24	3.4%
Nuclear	794	19.4%	199	1,068	18.8%
Renewables	360	8.8%	724	284	14.9%
			Total Subsidy Value[b]		
Biomass	40	1.0%	36		0.5%
Geothermal	15	0.4%	14		0.2%
Hydropower	258	6.3%	174		2.6%
Solar	1	0.0%	14		0.2%
Wind	31	0.8%	724		10.7%
Landfill Gas	6	0.1%	8		0.1%
Municipal Solid Waste	9	0.2%	1		0.0%
Transmission and Distribution	-i-		735	500	18.3%
Total	**4,091**	**100%**	**4,281**	**2,466**	**100%**

Source: Energy Information Administration (EIA), Federal Financial Interventions and Subsidies in Energy Markets 2007.

Notes: An "-i-" indicates that the value was found as "not meaningful" by the EIA. Columns may not sum due to rounding.

a. Other subsidies include direct expenditures, research and development expenditures, and federal electricity support.

b. The EIA does not distinguish between tax subsidies and other subsidies for specific renewable technologies.

In 2007, refined coal received a large share of federal financial support for electricity (32%) relative to the share of electricity produced using refined coal (1.8%). During 2007, synthetic (refined) coal was able to claim the tax credit for unconventional fuels under § 29 of the IRC. In response to concerns surrounding abuse, this credit was allowed to expire as scheduled at the end of 2007. Following expiration of this incentive, the 59 plants that had been producing synthetic coal ceased production.[40]

By 2010, renewables received the majority of direct federal financial support for electricity. The increase in the share of federal financial support for renewables is largely due to the Section 1603

---

[40] Energy Information Administration (EIA), Direct Federal Financial Interventions and Subsidies in Energy in Fiscal Year 2010, p. 11.

grants in lieu of tax credits program. Taxpayers that otherwise would have been eligible for the production tax credit (PTC), and would have received this tax credit over 10 years, may now choose to claim a one-time lump sum grant. In other words, much of the increase in share of federal financial support for renewables between 2007 and 2010 can be attributed to the change in the type of federal support being provided (tax credits paid out over time versus one-time grants) as opposed to real changes in the level of federal support being provided.[41]

The election to receive this one-time payment in 2010, rather than claim PTCs over a 10-year period, highlights the timing problem inherent in per-unit-of-production subsidy calculations. If all companies chose to take the PTC rather than the grant, the 2010 per-unit-of-production subsidy would appear lower than if all companies elected to receive a Section 1603 grant, even if the cost to the government of the PTC option were equal to the cost of the grant option. If the grant is allowed to expire as scheduled at the end of 2011, the share of federal financial support provided to renewables would be expected to fall substantially. Further, since projects that elected to receive the grant instead of tax credits will not be receiving tax credits in future years, the cost of supporting renewables will remain lower than if only tax credits had been available for 10 years following the grant's expiration.

The EIA studies also evaluate subsidies and support for energy that is not related to electricity production. EIA estimates that in 2010 (2007), $10.4 billion ($9.8 billion) of the $37.2 billion ($16.6 billion) in total energy-related subsidies supported non-electricity-related uses of energy. These subsidies include those that support the transportation sector, or fuels-related subsidies. Non-electricity-related energy subsidies also support primary end-use consumption or energy in the residential, commercial, and industrial sectors. **Table 6** and **Table 7** summarize the EIA's findings on energy subsidies relative to energy production for energy not related to electricity production.

Table 6. Energy Subsidies Not Related to Electricity Production, 2010

dollar values in millions

	Production		Federal Financial Incentives	
Fuel Type	Fuel Production Not Used For Electricity (quadrillion Btu)	% Total	Total Subsidies[a]	% Total
Coal	2.94	8.3%	169	1.6%
Natural Gas and Petroleum Liquids	28.55	80.3%	2,165	20.7%
Biomass / Biofuels	3.87	10.9%	7,646	73.2%
Geothermal	0.06	0.2%	73	0.7%
Solar	0.10	0.3%	169	1.6%
Other Renewables	0.02	0.0%	226	2.2%
Total	35.54	100%	10,448	100%

---

[41] For additional information on the Section 1603 grants in lieu of tax credits program, see CRS Report R41635, *ARRA Section 1603 Grants in Lieu of Tax Credits for Renewable Energy: Overview, Analysis, and Policy Options*, by Phillip Brown and Molly F. Sherlock.

Source: CRS and Energy Information Administration (EIA), Direct Federal Financial Interventions and Subsidies in Energy in Fiscal Year 2010.

Notes: Columns may not sum due to rounding.

a. The data as presented by EIA does not distinguish between tax and non-tax subsidies for energy not related to electricity production.

Most of the non-electricity-related energy produced in 2010, or consumed in 2007, came from natural gas or petroleum liquids.[42] The majority of federal financial support for non-electricity energy in both 2010 and 2007, however, was provided to biofuels (including non-electricity biomass and ethanol).

Although the results of the EIA study are not directly comparable to the analysis of federal tax support across different energy resources presented above, similar patterns emerge. Notably, although biofuels are responsible for a relatively small share of total energy production, relative to other fuels, biofuels receive a large share of federal financial support for energy. Relative to the share of energy produced using renewables, these resources also receive a disproportionate share of energy-related federal financial support. It is important to note, however, that this type of analysis does not indicate whether the distribution of federal financial support across various energy resources is consistent with energy policy goals. Energy policy may be designed to be consistent with certain national security, environmental, or economic objectives that might require that the distribution of federal financial support for energy not be aligned with the distribution of energy production across various energy resources.

Table 7. Energy Subsidies Not Related to Electricity Production, 2007

dollar values in millions

Fuel Type	Consumption		Federal Financial Incentives	
	Fuel Consumption not Used For Electricity (quadrillion Btu)	% Total	Total Subsidies[a]	% Total
Coal	1.93	3.2%	78	1.3%
Refined Coal	0.16	0.3%	214	3.4%
Natural Gas and Petroleum Liquids	55.78	91.5%	1,921	30.8%
Ethanol / Biofuels	0.57	0.9%	3,249	52.1%
Geothermal	0.04	0.1%	1	0.0%
Solar	0.07	0.1%	184	3.0%
Other Renewables	2.50	4.1%	360	5.8%
Hydrogen	-ii-		230	3.7%
Total (Fuel Specific)	**60.95**	**100%**	**6,237**	**100%**

---

[42] The 2007 EIA study looked at fuel consumption relative to non-electricity federal financial support for energy. The 2010 report instead looked at fuel production.

Source: Energy Information Administration (EIA), Federal Financial Interventions and Subsidies in Energy Markets 2007.

Notes: An "-ii-" indicates positive fuel consumption of less than 500 trillion Btu. Columns may not sum due to rounding.

a. The data as presented by EIA does not distinguish between tax and non-tax subsidies for energy not related to electricity production.

Concluding Remarks

The majority of energy produced in the U.S. continues to come from fossil energy sources. In recent years, the majority of energy tax incentives have served to benefit renewable energy resources. The data presented in this report illustrate that, relative to production levels, federal financial support for renewable energy exceeds support for fossil sources of energy. Roughly half of the support for renewable energy in 2010 benefitted biofuels. Since biofuels incentives have generally expired, without extension of expired incentives, there will be limited tax-related support for biofuels beyond 2012. Further, the expiration of the Section 1603 grants in lieu of tax credits program will reduce the share of tax-related support for renewables in future years.

Variation in the amount of federal financial support relative to energy produced across energy resources may be consistent with various environmental or economic objectives. For example, tax incentives designed to reduce reliance on imported petroleum may be consistent with energy security goals. Tax incentives that promote renewable energy resources may be consistent with certain environmental objectives. Energy tax incentives can also be used to support emerging technologies and encourage commercialization of high-risk innovations. While subsidy per unit of production or subsidy relative to production level calculations may provide a starting point for evaluating energy tax policy, a complete policy analysis should consider why the level of federal financial support might differ across various energy technologies.

Appendix A. Comparing Energy Production to Energy Tax Incentives: 2009

While the proportion of primary energy production attributable to certain energy resources changes slowly over time, there are often substantial changes in the estimated value of energy-related tax incentives for certain types of energy resources from year to year. For example, in 2009, 77.4% of energy-related tax incentives benefitted renewables (**Table A-1**). By 2010, the share of energy-related tax incentives attributable to renewables had declined to 68.1% (see **Table 3**). The primary reason for this decline is that in 2009, "black liquor" qualified for the alternative fuel mixture credit.[43] Thus, the tax expenditure estimate for tax credits for alcohol fuels was substantially higher in 2009 ($6.5 billion) than in 2010 ($0.1 billion). Annual changes in the estimated cost of energy-related tax incentives can result in substantial year-to-year changes in the proportion of energy-related tax incentives attributable to various energy resources.

Table A-1. Comparing Energy Production and Energy Tax Incentives: Fossil Fuels and Renewables
2009

	Production		Tax Incentives	
	Quadrillion Btu	% of Total	Billions of Dollars	% of Total
Fossil Fuels	56.9	77.9%	$2.5	12.6%
Renewables[a]	7.8	10.6%	$15.4	77.4%
Renewables (excluding hydro-electric)	*5.1*	*7.0%*	*$15.4[b]*	*77.4%[b]*
Renewables (excluding biofuels and related tax incentives)	*6.2*	*8.5%*	*$2.9*	*14.6%*
Renewables (excluding hydro-electric and biofuels and related tax incentives)	*3.5*	*4.8%*	*$2.9[b]*	*14.6%[b]*

Source: Calculated using data presented in **Table 1** and **Table 2** above.

a. Renewables tax incentives include targeted tax incentives designed to support renewable electricity and renewable fuels.

b. The value of total tax incentives for renewables excluding hydro-electric power is less than the total value of tax incentives when those available for hydro-power are included. However, the difference is small. JCT estimates that in 2009, the tax expenditures for qualified hydropower under the PTC are less than $50 million. During 2009, one award of $4.1 million was paid to a hydropower facility under the Section 1603 grant program. Hydropower has also received less in CREB financing than was awarded to solar and wind technologies. During 2009, the tax expenditure for CREBs was less than $50 million across all technologies.

---

[43] For more information, see CRS Report R41769, *Energy Tax Policy: Issues in the 112th Congress*, by Molly F. Sherlock and Margot L. Crandall-Hollick.

Appendix B. An Alternative Method for Evaluating the Value of Energy Tax Incentives Across Technologies: The Effective Tax Rate Approach

Another way to measure the relative subsidization of various energy resources is to use an effective tax rate approach. Effective tax rates, in the context presented below, are used to evaluate how the tax system affects incentives for capital investment. Lower effective tax rates on capital investment can promote investment in certain sectors.

The remainder of this section summarizes the results of a 2010 study analyzing energy-related tax incentives and investment.[44] This study uses the 2007 tax code to evaluate its impact on the inventive to invest in different types of energy capital. As was the case with the EIA study presented above, the effective tax rate analysis here does not incorporate energy tax policy changes under ARRA. Nonetheless, this analysis highlights the incentives for investment created by provisions in the tax code related to energy investment and production.

What Is an "Effective" Tax Rate

The effective tax rates measures the impact of the tax system on investment decisions. In the context of this report, an effective tax rate is defined as $\frac{\rho - r}{\rho}$. In this equation, ρ is the real before-tax return on the marginal investment and r is the real return paid to investors.[45] Assume that investors require an after-tax rate of return of 6% for a given investment. Assume next that a project must have a real before-tax rate of return of 9% to cover taxes, depreciation, and payments to investors. Under these conditions, the effective tax rate would be 33%.[46] Negative effective tax rates indicate that the tax code is actually subsidizing investment to the point where taxpayers are willing to accept a before-tax rate of return that is less than the after-tax rate of return for an investment.

Effective tax rates provide a single measure for the impact of the tax system on capital investments. Thus, there are many provisions in the tax code that can affect effective tax rates. In the energy sector, depreciation rules, investment and production tax incentives, and tax rules specific to the oil and gas sector are all important in the calculation of effective tax rates.

Effective Tax Rates for Energy-Related Capital Investments

Effective tax rates in the energy sector suggest that the tax code provides greater incentives for certain types of energy-related capital investments. In 2007, the tax code created the largest incentive for capital investment in solar thermal energy generation facilities. In 2007, solar

---

[44] Gilbert E. Metcalf, "Investment in Energy Infrastructure and the Tax Code," in *Tax Policy and the Economy*, ed. Jeffery R. Brown, 24 ed. (The University of Chicago Press, 2010), pp. 1-33.

[45] For additional details on the effective tax rate methodology, see Congressional Budget Office, *Taxing Capital Income: Effective Rates and Approaches to Reform*, October 2005.

[46] Using the effective tax rate formula given in the text, the effective tax rate is calculated as (0.09-0.06) / 0.09 = 0.333.

benefitted from a 30% investment tax credit as well as five-year accelerated depreciation. The 2007 effective tax rate for capital investments in solar thermal was estimated at -244.7% (see **Table B-1**). Wind, which benefitted from the production tax credit (PTC) as well as five-year accelerated depreciation, was estimated to face an effective tax rate of -163.8%. These effective tax rates suggest that the tax code creates strong incentives for direct capital investment in wind and solar energy resources. Overall, the effective tax rates for renewables and nuclear are substantially lower than the effective tax rates for coal and gas. Empirical evidence suggests that energy-related investments may in fact be influenced by tax incentives. Metcalf (2010) finds that investment in wind capacity is "strongly influenced by tax policy."

Table B-1. Effective Tax Rates for Energy-Related Capital Investments
2007

	2007 Law	No Tax Credits	Economic Depreciation
Electric Utilities: Generation			
Nuclear	-99.5	32.4	-49.4
Coal (Pulverized Coal)	38.9	38.9	39.3
Coal (IRCC)	-11.6	38.9	-10.3
Gas	34.4	34.4	39.3
Wind	-163.8	12.8	-13.7
Solar Thermal	-244.7	12.8	-26.5
Petroleum			
Oil Drilling, Non-Integrated	-13.5	-13.5	39.3
Oil Drilling, Integrated	15.2	15.2	39.3
Refining[a]	19.1	19.1	39.3
Natural Gas			
Gathering Pipelines	15.4	15.4	39.3
Other Pipelines	27.0	27.0	39.3

Source: Gilbert E. Metcalf, "Investment in Energy Infrastructure and the Tax Code," in *Tax Policy and the Economy*, ed. Jeffery R. Brown, 24 ed. (The University of Chicago Press, 2010), pp. 1-33.

Notes:

a. The effective tax rate on refining capital reflects the 50% expensing allowance available in 2007 for investments in additional refinery capacity.

Provisions in the tax code may distort investment decisions for other types of energy resources. The effective tax rate for capital investment in nuclear electric generation (-99.5%) also provides strong investment incentives. The Energy Policy Act of 2005 (EPACT05; P.L. 109-58) introduced a production tax credit for new commercial nuclear reactors.[47] Despite these incentives, new nuclear facilities have been slow to develop.[48]

---

[47] An effective tax rate analysis published by Ernst & Young estimates the effective tax rate for nuclear energy capital to be 26.7%. The difference between this estimate and that provided by Metcalf (2010) stems from the different treatment of the nuclear PTC enacted as part of EPACT05. See Ernst & Young, *International Comparison of* (continued...)

Various tax incentives available to the oil and gas industry also influence effective tax rates on oil and gas investment. Effective tax rates on investments made by non-integrated oil and gas firms are lower than for integrated firms.[49] The primary reason for this difference is that non-integrated producers are able to fully expense intangible drilling costs (IDCs) and are able to take advantage of percentage depletion. Integrated producers can only expense 70% of IDCs and must claim cost rather than percentage depletion.

Author Contact Information

Molly F. Sherlock
Specialist in Public Finance
msherlock@crs.loc.gov, 7-7797

(...continued)
Depreciation Rules and Tax Rates for Selected Energy Investments, May 2, 2007, available at http://www.accf.org/media/dynamic/8/media_82.pdf.

[48] For additional background, see CRS Report RL33558, *Nuclear Energy Policy*, by Mark Holt.

[49] The effective tax rate is also influenced by the price of oil and operating profits in the industry. The figures reported here are those that were presented in Metcalf (2010).

www.ingramcontent.com/pod-product-compliance
Lightning Source LLC
Chambersburg PA
CBHW081246180526
45171CB00005B/563